## JACK THORNE

Jack Thorne's other plays for the stage include adaptations of *Let the Right One In* (National Theatre of Scotland at Dundee Rep, the Royal Court and the Apollo Theatre, London, 2013/14) and *Stuart: A Life Backwards* (Underbelly, Edinburgh and tour, 2013); *Mydidae* (Soho, 2012; Trafalgar Studios, 2013); an adaptation of Friedrich Dürrenmatt's *The Physicists* (Donmar Warehouse, 2012); *Bunny* (Underbelly, Edinburgh, 2010; Soho, 2011); *2nd May 1997* (Bush, 2009); *When You Cure Me* (Bush, 2005; Radio 3's Drama on Three, 2006); *Fanny and Faggot* (Pleasance, Edinburgh, 2004 and 2007; Finborough, 2007; English Theatre of Bruges, 2007; Trafalgar Studios, 2007); and *Stacy* (Tron, 2006; Arcola, 2007; Trafalgar Studios, 2007). His radio plays include *Left at the Angel* (Radio 4, 2007), an adaptation of *The Hunchback of Notre Dame* (2009) and an original play *People Snogging in Public Places* (Radio 3's Wire slot, 2009). He was a core writer in all three series of *Skins* (E4, Channel 4, BBC America), writing five episodes. His other TV writing includes *The Fades* (2012 BAFTA for Best Drama Series), *Shameless, Cast-Offs, This is England '86* (2011 Royal Television Society Award for Best Writer – Drama), *This is England '88, This is England '90* and the thirty-minute drama *The Spastic King*. His work for film includes the features *A Long Way Down*, adapted from Nick Hornby's novel, and *The Scouting Book for Boys*, which won him the Star of London Best Newcomer Award at the London Film Festival 2009.

**Other Titles in this Series**

Jack Thorne

# BURYING YOUR BROTHER IN THE PAVEMENT

## NICK HERN BOOKS

London

www.nickhernbooks.co.uk

**A Nick Hern Book**

*Burying Your Brother in the Pavement* first published as a single edition paperback in Great Britain in 2014 by Nick Hern Books Limited, The Glasshouse, 49a Goldhawk Road, London W12 8QP

*Burying Your Brother in the Pavement* copyright © 2014 Jack Thorne

Jack Thorne has asserted his right to be identified as the author of this work

Cover image © Shutterstock.com/Iakov Filimonov

Designed and typeset by Nick Hern Books, London
Printed in Great Britain by Mimeo Ltd, Cambridgeshire PE29 6XX

A CIP catalogue record for this book is available from the British Library

ISBN    978 1 84842 416 6

**Woodland**
**CARBON**
www.woodlandcarbon.co.uk
NICK HERN BOOKS
Printed on Carbon Captured paper

*Burying Your Brother in the Pavement* was commissioned as part of the 2008 National Theatre Connections Festival and premiered by youth theatres across the UK, including a performance at the National Theatre in July 2008.

Each year the National Theatre asks ten writers to create new plays to be performed by young theatre companies all over the country. From Scotland to Cornwall and Northern Ireland to Norfolk, Connections celebrates great new writing for the stage – and the energy, commitment and talent of young theatremakers.

www.nationaltheatre.org.uk/connections

**Characters**

TOM
MR WILKINS
COURTNEY
BOY SOPRANO
AUNTIE HELEN
FRIENDLY PHIL
UNCLE GERRY
TIGHT
MARTIN
LUKE
BILL
SIMON
SANDRA
LEO
LIBBY
RICKY
JK
DRUNK BILL
DAVID McPHEE
MISS HANDS
PUSHCHAIR MUM
BABYFATHER
ESTATE AGENT
STAN
CLIENT
PC BOB
PC BILL
UNDERWEAR MAN

*And* MOTHERS, FURNITURE PEOPLE, SCHOOLKIDS

## Production Notes

The cast can be as large as a stage can contain, or as small as five.

Aside from Tom, Tight, Luke and Courtney, the parts are non-gender specific. No parts are racially specific.

There is no score, and so be encouraged to do and try everything with the music. It would be brilliant to have either live music or have someone mixing sound live onstage with the actors. The more the musicians or the sound guy can be bought into the action, the better.

The most important thing is that this play is kept scruffy – nothing is beautiful – everything is quick and swiftly accomplished. This should look like a piece of theatre achieved on the bounce and stuffed full of life. This means two things – one, if you happen to have a brilliant rollerblader in your cast, then use her – and add a triple-Lutz somersault to the Dairylea song number. Equally, don't let the technical overwhelm: I specify a lot of spotlights in the first few pages, but these could easily be torches held up to people's faces, and, in fact, might work better like that. Scene changes should be incorporated into the action. All the stage and auditorium should be used.

## Production References

Robbie Williams was a popular entertainer in post-war Britain. Jesus Christ was less popular, but equally entertaining in pre-war Galilee. Planning Law is both popular and entertaining.

## One

*It's dark. Very dark indeed.*

TOM *lights a torch. A pathetic torch. But it's almost blinding in this darkness.*

*As our eyes adjust, we take in his surroundings… He's underneath a table. A small table that he's had to squeeze himself underneath of. The table is in a large dusty attic.*

TOM *is an ordinary-looking teenager in his early teens. He is wearing the hand-me-downs of a cooler older brother. But he wears them slightly wrong. Too many buttons done up on a polo shirt, that sort of thing…*

TOM. I first had the idea that I was the son of God, when I was nine.

I'd just read the Bible.

Not the whole Bible, not cover-to-cover but – you know… extensive dipping… Anyway, the more I read, the more it sort of made sense, that I was the second coming. Jesus Christ. Two.

The sequel.

I mean, my mum a virgin? Well, looking at her you could certainly believe so. Check. Dad not my real dad? We never did have much in common. Check. Me leading a sad-and-tortured-life-where-everyone-hates-me-and-I-have-to-die-for -the-good-of-humanity-who'll-be-sorry-when-I'm-gone?

Check.

But then I tried to cure a leper – well, a kid with really bad eczema… it didn't work. He just bled a lot. I tried to – rip some of his skin off and…

*Beat.*

I first got the idea I might have Aids after a particularly aggressive sex-ed class – you know, the sort of class where your teacher just repeatedly shouts –

*Spotlight on a harassed-looking teacher, in a tatty-looking blazer. He's spitty.*

MR WILKINS. You must NEVER have sex. Never. Ever. Ever.

*Spotlight off.*

TOM. I mean, talk about premature, I hadn't even persuaded a girl to kiss me yet. But he always was premature, Mr Wilkins.

*Spotlight on* MR WILKINS *inflagrante (tastefully) with a blow-up doll.*

MR WILKINS. I'm not normally like that. I'm a good lover, really I am… oh, don't look like that…

*The blow-up doll looks back, the same open-mouthed expression on its face it always has.*

TOM. So Aids – me? Unlikely! But then I had a tetanus shot and it took them ages to find a vein and I thought – well, maybe I had a mutated version of Aids – the sort where you don't get to do anything good to catch it. 'I caught mine through drugs.' 'I caught mine through sex.' 'I just, well, I just sort of got it.' 'Why?' 'Because I'm unlucky.'

There are loads of other examples – the time I thought I'd developed a cure for blindness in biology class because I seemed to be able to see things with my eyes closed – the time when I thought I may have inadvertently started a war between Korea and the Isle of Sheppey with some stuff I'd written on my blog – the time when I thought I'd accidentally castrated my dog –

*A dog howls in the distance.* TOM *frowns.*

Okay, well, I sort of did castrate my dog. That's a long story… my point is this…

It's normal to be centre of your own world, in your head, star of your… and me… I don't just star in my head, I kind of

suffocate all other forms of life. But this – finally – I've got
the opportunity to actually be some kind of star and I'm –

TOM *hears something. He freezes and turns off the light. He
indicates to us silence, takes a deep breath and holds it.*

COURTNEY *opens up a hatch in the attic floor and light
immediately spills into the room. She looks around
aggressively with a torch of her own.*

COURTNEY. Tom… Tom? If you're up here, you little turd…

*The light passes across* TOM, *his face is racked with fear.*

Tom? Don't be a shit okay?

*She twirls the torch through one more tour. It sees nothing.*

No, turd's not in the loft, Dad…

*She closes the hatch. And the light goes with it. We're back
in the dark.*

TOM *breathes out, counts to three, steadies himself, opens
his eyes and then turns on the torch again.*

TOM. They're a – having a funeral downstairs.

I'm supposed to be there. Down there. With them.

I mean, it's not like a guy missing his own wedding – I
mean, it's not my funeral, obviously – TA-DAH! I'm alive –
so, but… still… I'm expected to be there. And not here –
hiding under a table in my attic.

*He chews a finger and looks contemplative.*

Luke – my brother – always used to come up here when he
was upset. I was – too afraid – always thought there was
something living up here. Something swimming in the water
tank, sliding through the pipes, nestling in the insulation. But
now – well –

TOM *looks around. He shines the torch around.*

Funerals – fun-e-rals – rals from the Latin meaning 'the rule
is'. The rule… is fun. Great news for my little cousin Kevin,

who has jam around his mouth and mayonnaise in his hair and likes randomly launching into his world-famous impression of Robbie Williams. And less good news for my mum who just wants to cry – on me.

*Spotlight on a* MOTHER, *in tears.* TOM *looks at her carefully. She looks up at* TOM.

*They hold for maybe fifteen seconds, just looking at each other. Then the spotlight flicks off and* TOM *is staring into blackness.*

My brother died. Badly. It's that simple really…

*He chews a finger and looks contemplative.*

You know why they call them wakes? It used to be a time when people sat by the body waiting to see if it woke up. Before doctors knew what they were doing. Some bodies did wake up – in which case they were alive and mourning was kind of pointless – others didn't – in which case… well… Either way, everyone got drunk.

I know that I can't stay here. I didn't mean to – I was panicked up here when an auntie I barely knew, licked my face and told me I was a good boy and then tried to give me a deep-fried-mushroom thing from Iceland. And it…

Jesus didn't have to deal with this rubbish, did he?

TOM *looks around. He shines the torch around.*

I need to get out of here. I mean… here. I mean, all of here. I mean, the house… I mean, the funeral… I need to get out.

*He waits a second and then turns out his torch.*

*Silence.*

*Slowly light spreads across the stage, to reveal a typical middle-class living room. Knick-knacks, paddy-whacks, comfortable sofas and too many standing lights, the room is musty and filled with gloom.*

*A lad – preferably a* BOY SOPRANO – *steps out alone into the centre of the room. He takes a moment to compose himself. He has a small cough to himself. He sits on a stool in the centre of the space. He opens his mouth to sing. But thinks better of it.*

*He gets off the stool and walks over to the sideboard. There is a glass of water on it. He drinks from it. He sits back on the stool. He opens his mouth to sing. But thinks better of it. He opens a drawer from the telephone stand and pulls out a fork. He clinks the fork against the glass. It makes a ringing noise.*

*He opens his mouth to sing. But thinks better of it. He drinks some more from the glass. He pulls out the fork and clinks it again. Again it rings, but this time at a slightly higher pitch. A pitch that reverbs around the audience. He smiles. That's the note he was looking for.*

*'When Your Brother's Dead'. A music-hall number.*

BOY (*sings*).
> When your brother's dead
> Your mouth should taste of lead
> And your eyes should feel
> Like marbles.
>
> So when that's not the case
> You have to fake your face
> To make relatives believe you're
> A good boy
>
> And while everyone cries
> You quickly rub your eyes
> To make them red like everyone
> Else's
>
> And you shut out
> The niggling in your snout
> That you're a nasty bastard
> With no feelings

Cossssssssssssssssssssssssssssssssssssssss –

*He holds the note a very long time... He touches an item of furniture onstage. A light fitting. It grows into a MAN. A normal-looking MAN wearing a light-shade for a hat.*

*The* MAN *joins the* BOY *singing. The song is sung slower now.*

When your brother's dead –

*And a candlestick holder is touched, and similarly grows into a* MAN, *with candlesticks for hands. Slowly we discover that all the furniture is similarly alive. Think* Beauty and the Beast. *Or Ikea on a school night.*

Your mouth should taste of lead –

*And another voice joins in. And a sofa unfolds itself to reveal a baritone within.*

And your eyes should feel
Like marbles –

*And slowly the stage fills with people. All dressed as items of furniture. Soprano telephones, and tenor televisions, the stage is suddenly a very exciting place.*

So when that's not the case
You have to fake your face –

TOM *appears at the side of the stage and begins to attempt to surreptitiously move through the throng.*

AUNTIE HELEN (*a bookcase*). TOM! We've found you! I've found Tom, everyone! How are you bearing up? Such a lovely boy… Such a loss… vol-au-vent? Mini-quiche?

TOM *wilts. She turns him around do-si-do style.*

To make relatives believe you're
A good boy –

*And now the cast start to dance, a slightly hypnotic waltz. The stage is alive with lights and furniture people. All waltzing around the stage. All pushing and prodding* TOM *as they do. Who is now desperate to escape them.*

FRIENDLY PHIL (*a rug*). TOM. Where did you disappear to? Need a hug? Feeling left out. Wishing it was you?

And while everyone cries
You quickly rub your eyes

To make them red like everyone
Else's –

UNCLE GERRY (*a painting*). TOM! Your brother dead. You live? Where's the punchline?

TOM *begins to scrabble through, he scrabbles under and out of the mêlée. And the mourners transform into passing trees and cars and people – he runs through them all, desperate for freedom. All the while the singing gets more intense. A descant is put into effect, and a base line and a tenor line. It sounds kind of great, a wonderful swelling noise.*

And you try to shut out
The niggling in your snout
That you're a nasty bastard
With no feelings
With no feelings
Wwwith no feeeeelings…

*Finally* TOM *manages to escape and runs from the pursuing furniture, out of which* COURTNEY *slips.*

COURTNEY (*stays as* COURTNEY). Tom! Tom. TOM!

*He turns, looks at her a second, and then turns back to fleeing. And then suddenly everyone falls flat. Taking all remaining props down with them.*

*And* TOM *is free.*

*And breathless, and confused.*

## Two

*A wet summer's night. Not that it is wet now but it has been. The weather feels intense.* TOM *is sitting on a wall.*

TOM *isn't sure why he's there.*

TOM (*as he catches his breath*). I've always liked running. I'm not fast but I like it. It makes me feel weightless and numb and I like being out of breath. And I've always liked stopping – and that feeling where your blood suddenly surges all over your body – where the numbness gets replaced with something else… But I never expected to stop here…

*He clicks his fingers, a light snare drum plays, and the cast lying on the floor stand up.*

The Tunstall Estate.

*The men in the chorus flick up their suit-jacket collars. They look like 1930s gangsters now.*

Not a –

*The chorus exit in different directions, with a sort of menace.*

Well, not a place many would choose to run to. Choose to run from, yes. But run to? No.

We did a school local-history project on the Tunstall. In the 1950s believe it or not this was a place of hope, somewhere where you – but that changed. Rot problem. They didn't build the estate on the right land you see and, so some of the foundations sunk, uh… And then they had problems with the riots…

TOM *stops talking.*

*A young lad* (TIGHT) *walks across the stage, listening to some R&B on his mobile phone.*

*He doesn't stop, he doesn't look at* TOM.

*When he's left,* TOM – *scared by this kid* – *checks he's gone and counts to three.*

The 1980s riots – all electrical appliances, including lighting fixtures were ripped out and no one really replaced them right... And now they're –

TOM *stops talking again.*

*The young lad has reappeared at the side of the stage.*

*He looks at* TOM *closely.* TOM *tries to act casual.*

TIGHT. You hands-free or you just talking to you?

TOM. What?

TIGHT (*slow, as if talking to a foreigner*). You hands-free or you just talking to you?

TOM. Oh, uh, no... I was talking to myself... sorry...

TIGHT *considers this thought.*

TIGHT. Riiiiiight.

TIGHT *nods and exits.*

TOM *counts to three.*

TOM. The 1980s riots –

TIGHT *re-enters.*

TIGHT *thinks and then approaches* TOM, *with a pimp roll.*
TIGHT *thinks he knows where it's at. He's wrong, he has no idea where it's at. But he's kind of sweet.*

TIGHT (*under his breath*). You wanna buy a Travelcard?

TOM. What?

TIGHT. I got some Travelcards, you wanna buy one?

TOM. No. I'm okay.

TIGHT. Give you great price?

TOM. No. I just, I'd rather be – on my own –

TIGHT. I ain't a generous guy normal. I am known round here as 'Tight' cos I'm like... tight. But for you – my business associates would literally kill me for this – but I could be prepared – on this occasion, and on this occasion only, to give wholesale prices, just cos – well – you look like a kid who just got given a teddy and realised it's full of used syringes and condoms –

TOM (*starting to get annoyed*). A kid? How old are you?

TIGHT (*cough*). How old I look?

TOM. I don't know... fourteen.

TIGHT (*high*). I never do! (*Coughs so as to speak lower and manly.*) I never do. I mean, sixteen, yeah, I'd buy sixteen if you were offering. But fourteen? You are talking to a guy who like regular – reg-u-lar – gets served for Marlboro Lights.

TOM. How old are you though?

TIGHT *considers*.

TIGHT. Fourteen. But that ain't the point.

TOM *says nothing*.

You sure about the Travelcard?

TOM. Look. I don't know who you are. And... and... Just. *Leave me alone, will you?*

TIGHT. I would... but I'm too nice. This ain't the place for a boy like you. Take a Travelcard, go somewhere better. I mean, boy 'bout your age got stabbed here less than a week ago. With a bottle. You know what I'm saying?

TOM. Yeah.

TIGHT. I mean, you is in Tunstall land now, this place is the definition of rough – look rough up in your dictionary, you'd get a photo of this place. I mean, we is basically sitting on a murder scene here, serious! This area supposed to have all dem 'police don't cross' signs and stuff round it. Yellow tape you know, with the black stripes, looks pretty cool, yeah? But someone nicked it. That's how dangerous this area is – we don't just get told we're dangerous, we nick the tape that tells us it. Rah!

TOM. Right.

*TIGHT thinks, coughs, and then tries anyway.*

TIGHT. You don't want any 'police don't cross' yellow tape, do you? Cos I just happened to come into a little bit of it myself recently. Very good price.

TOM. I'm okay.

TIGHT. But you won't stay here, yeah? It's too – it's not right for a boy like you – here..

TOM. What is a boy like me?

TIGHT. No offence, but a posh boy…

TOM (*offended*). I'm not posh! I go to my local school… comprehensive school…

TIGHT. But you're in top-set maths, I can tell… and your school is one of dem nice ones – still free and that – but you don't get kids like me going…

*TOM thinks.*

TOM. Thanks, for being worried and everything, but I kind of got to stay here.

TIGHT. Why? You broke your legs? Cos they look fine to me.

TOM. My brother was killed here, last week. Stabbed with a bottle.

*That's shocked TIGHT.*

TIGHT. Oh.

TOM. Yeah.

*Pause.*

I just, I wanted to come here and… I don't know…

TIGHT. You – his brother? No, you ain't.

TOM. Um. Well, yeah… I am…

*TIGHT grabs TOM's face to study it. Harder than he should do.*

TIGHT. You don't even look like him.

TOM (*ping*). Hang on… You knew him?

TIGHT *stops again. He's spotted something – something beautiful. He stares at* TOM *now. He lets go of* TOM*'s face.*

TIGHT (*soft*). Just then – okay. Yeah, just then. When the lamp caught your face just then… Yeah, I can see it…

TOM. How did you know him?

TIGHT *thinks. Processes. And considers. You can almost see the cogs turn.*

TIGHT. I gotta go. Got fifteen Travelcards to pimp before the last Tube runs – and these Oysters, man, they're playing with my trade. Still – (*Takes a golden card out of his pocket and blows it clean of dust.*) want you to have this. (*Points to various things on it.*) My mobile. My pager. My only-to-be-called-in-extreme-emergencies-cos-my-mum-gets-well-mad-when-my-mates-ring-the-house number. People know me as Tight – or – if you're speaking to my mum – Tre – but you don't get to call me Tre – cos no one does – I'm just saying, case you speak to her, you know?

TOM. How did you know him? Please. Tell me.

TIGHT *considers telling him, but decides against it.*

TIGHT. You need anything. Anything. I mean, I ain't gonna get you stuff for free. But you know, give you a good price. Cos look… Laters.

TOM. Hang on – how did you know my brother? Please. PLEASE!

TIGHT *thinks, and then rolls off the stage. But the walk is less confident now. He hesitates and turns around one final time before making his exit.*

TIGHT. Another time, bro, another time…

*And then he finally goes.*

TOM *sits back on his wall. He looks around, he shivers…*

**Three**

*The sound of a baby crying. Not wailing, but snuffling, making noise, doing what babies do. In the background the sun is setting. Maybe a few windows are opened and today's washing brought in from the night sky. The smells of cooking dinner are brought out, and there are some exotic tastes out there. Sausages from one kitchen mix with saffron from another and sage from another as well.*

TOM *is staring at the ground, he looks up at the audience, astonished.*

TOM. There's a stain on the ground. I didn't notice it when I first… a bloodstain I think.

*He bends down as if to touch it, but pulls his hand away. He looks at his hand.*

Maybe I'm supposed to be solving the case. I always thought I'd be a good policeman. You know, a maverick one. Like Columbo. Or Dennis Waterman. Maybe I'm here to solve my brother's murder and go home to my parents the conquering hero on the back of a white unicorn…

Or maybe I'm here to make people feel bad. This is a pretty open place to die at, isn't it? Someone must have heard or seen – my brother dying… Maybe I'm a torch to shine and pressure and… make the people who live here apologise and then I'll go home to my parents on the back of a white –

Or maybe I'm nothing. Just a mixed-up kid sitting on a cold wall. Looking at a – stain on the ground.

*He sniffs, it's cold now.*

We were ten months apart. Which means, as my friend Martin put it –

MARTIN *stands up from the audience.*

MARTIN. Must have got pregnant the first take. First take. Cos women, yeah, they won't let you sleep with them just after they have a baby. So… your dad must be potent. Po-tent. You know what I'm saying?

TOM. Martin doesn't have many friends. Nor do I. We're in
    computer club together. We run computer club. We're the
    founder members… We're the only members. And no, he
    doesn't really know what potent means…

MARTIN *sticks his thumb up at anyone who looks, and then
sits down again with a smile.*

We weren't supposed to be in the same year – me and Luke.
It's just, I got put forward a year. Mum wanted Luke to be
put forward a year too – for sort of – for symmetry. But they
pointed out he wasn't clever enough…

It sort of made sense… because up till then we'd always… I
mean, he'd sat in the cot beside me, he sat in the pushchair,
he'd only just finished breastfeeding when I started clamping.
He – he was always there to copy – when he started walking, I
started walking, when he squeezed his first word out, well, I'd
seen how he'd did it. I mean, I think that's why I got put
forward a year… I was just… copying. And now –

*A kid – LUKE – steps out onto the stage. He walks around
beside TOM.*

*They begin to move in time with each other, just a really
simple mirroring dance, framed under lights. Underneath, a
refrain of 'When Your Brother's Dead' is gently hummed by
the chorus from the wings.*

When he's –

LUKE *falls flat,* TOM *continues dancing for a moment until
he realises he's alone. Then he stops and looks at where*
LUKE *fell.*

Killed by a bottle. What do you do then? Who do you race
then? If racing's all you're used to, that is –

*Slowly people come onstage and throw down flowers where*
LUKE *lies. As if leaving flowers at a road-traffic accident.
Some from the audience, some from the stage,* MARTIN *also
approaches from where he was sitting.*

BILL. They were really different. I mean, they did everything
    different.

MARTIN. Tom was more… academic.

SIMON. Geek. He was a geek. And he looked so neeky man. He kind of breathed neeky. You know? Like, I don't know even how neeky breathes – but kinda lemony you know?

SANDRA. Luke was hot, I know they were s'posed to look similar, brothers and… But – they was living proof of it ain't what you got it's how you use it. And Tom – no offence – used nuffink.

LEO. Luke was in a band, you know? Tom was in computer club, you know?

MARTIN. It was the way Tom wore his shoes. It was everything. I mean, I'm not criticising…

SANDRA. It was the way Luke swung his hips.

LIBBY. It was the way Luke opened his baby blues.

RICKY. He just had something – Luke did…

*The* KIDS *pick up* LUKE *and carry him like a coffin, on their shoulders.*

TOM *watches them as they do.*

MARTIN. It'd have evened out in time. I mean, Tom was going to go to university. He definitely would have got there. And I'm not sure Luke would have…

SANDRA. Luke was exciting. Such a rubbish word. But –

MARTIN. It would have evened up in the end.

*They exit the stage, carrying* LUKE.

SANDRA. Just cos you're a geek too…

MARTIN. Not as bad a geek as Tom is…

SANDRA. No one's as bad as Tom is…

TOM *stares off to where* LUKE *has been taken. Still not sure how to react.*

**Four**

*It's night now. The milky-black of a street-lit night. The sort of
night where you can smell the pollution of the day.*

TOM *takes off his jacket, sits down beside the wall, and tries to
use his jacket as a blanket.*

TOM. I don't know how many people have tried sleeping on the
    street. A pavement for a mattress, a wall for a pillow, a jacket
    for your duvet. It isn't easy. And I don't know how many
    have tried sleeping on the Tunstall Estate but it's… loud –
    and – more awake at odder hours – and there's a smell too, a
    smell of anything can happen here…

*Somewhere in the distance a dog barks, a car engine revs
and a bottle is smashed.*

JK. OI!… COME BACK!

*JK comes running onto the stage.*

DRUNK BILL *comes from the back of the auditorium.*

DRUNK BILL (*singing*).
    I'm a tramp, and they love me…

*He swigs from a bottle and smiles and then faints dead away.*

TOM. And I don't know how many people have ever tried
    sleeping on the exact spot where their brother died. But
    it's… tricky. I mean, I don't even care he died, or I don't
    seem to, but I still get… And I'm too old for fairy tales, but I
    still get pavement elephants –

*The sound of an elephant trumpeting.*

– coming to trample me, and sky dragons –

*The sound of a dragon exclaiming.*

– come to –

COURTNEY. WHAT – ARE – YOU – DOING?

*TOM sits up with a start, and wipes his eyes.*

WHAT – are – YOU – DOING?

TOM *wakes with a stretch and immediately flinches when he sees his sister.*

TOM. Oh. Um. Hi. Courtney.

COURTNEY. WHAT ARE YOU DOING?

TOM. I was – sleeping – I think…

COURTNEY. It's three a.m.!

TOM. I reckon it's more normal to be asleep at three a.m. than shouting.

COURTNEY. You just ran off. Mum and Dad have been ringing round the hospital wards for the last three hours. They thought you'd done something stupid.

TOM. Well, I haven't.

COURTNEY. YES YOU HAVE! Luke's funeral and you pull this stunt. What? Worried you weren't getting enough attention…?

TOM. It's not about that.

COURTNEY. *Don't* try and pretend you cared about him… You hated each other.

TOM. I know.

COURTNEY. So why are you here?

TOM. I don't know. Felt right.

COURTNEY *picks him up by the arm and starts pulling him offstage.*

What are you doing? OI! OI!

COURTNEY. You're COMING WITH ME.

TOM. LET ME GO, COURTNEY. OR I'LL SCREAM.

COURTNEY *thinks and then screams, an ear-piercing scream. And then she screams again.*

COURTNEY. RAPE! RAPE!

*They look around the estate, not the slightest attempt has been made to help the damsel in distress.* COURTNEY *looks at* TOM *with a world-weary grin.*

Some good it'll do, screaming round here.

*She picks up his arm and starts pulling him off again.*

TOM. LET GO! LET GO! COURT!

*He pulls her hair in an attempt to get away from her, and not a light pull, but a full-hearted yank. She immediately responds by kicking at him. They throw each other onto the floor and have a fight. And yes – it's boy vs girl but it's also brother vs sister and so it's sort of okay. And she twists and she turns him but finally he pins her to the ground. Both are breathless.*

Submit?… Submit?

COURTNEY. Well, would you look at that. My little brother, finally able to beat his sister up…

TOM. Submit?

COURTNEY. No.

TOM. SUBMIT?

COURTNEY *considers her predicament.*

COURTNEY. Okay. Submit.

*He loosens his grip on her slightly.*

*She wriggles out a little.* TOM *tries to explain – softly.*

TOM. I need to stay here, okay? Will you tell them that. I know you don't understand, but I really need to stay here, okay?

*Now he fully lets go of her. She stands up and brushes herself down.*

COURTNEY. Can't believe you beat up a girl. Actually, can't believe you beat up anyone.

TOM. I know.

*Pause. She finally looks at him with compassion.*

COURTNEY. You are…? You are… okay… aren't you? I mean, not mental or…

TOM. Yeah. I'm okay… Will you… tell them where I am?

COURTNEY *considers. She looks around, she shivers.*

COURTNEY. Of all the places to choose to go… No. I won't tell them. It'll only hurt them. But I'll say you're safe. They'll shout at me to get me to tell… But I won't… You got three days, okay? Three days to get home, or I'll tell them exactly where you are and I don't care who it hurts. Deal?

TOM. Deal. Thanks.

*She hesitates and then exits.* TOM *thinks, and then takes off his jacket and readies himself for sleep again.*

And for some reason, sleeping becomes a lot easier after you've beaten up your older sister. A lot easier. No pavement elephants…

*An elephant sounds.* TOM *frowns.*

*No* pavement elephants. No… nothing…

TOM *is asleep.*

*Blackout.*

## Five

*The gentle mist of eight a.m. Windows open and the sound of radios being tuned and then blared out sound around the estate. Maybe a seven-year-old having a screaming fit after being told of Teletubby massacres also massages our eardrums.*

TOM *sleeps through this. He's a good pavement sleeper.*

*A line of* SCHOOLKIDS *come out from the wings and either stand on or by the wall. Preferably they should span the width of the stage.*

*They wake* TOM *with a start.*

*'Dairylea'. A marching song.*

THE SCHOOL CHORUS.
School – school – School – school –
School – school – School – school –
School – school – School – school –
School – school – School – school –
Scho-sch-sch-sch-school.

TOM *wipes his face with his hand and tries to get awake. And actually, it's not as difficult as he thought. He wakes easily. But he is slightly bewildered by all the noise.*

TOM. The Tunstall Estate at day is very different from the Tunstall at night. Filled with noise and colour, it's quite the place to be. Night is about the people who come out at night, day is about the mothers…

*The* MOTHERS, *with tea towels nattily tied around their heads like headscarves, come on singing. They are carrying brushes with which they brush in symmetry with one another. And maybe a few of these* MOTHERS *are men, and maybe they aren't. The* SCHOOL CHORUS *continues underneath throughout.*

MOTHERS.
He was twelve
When he said
He'd have nothing on his bread.

But Dairylea
Dairylea – (*Repeated in overlap by other* MOTHERS.)

TOM. And, despite my pavement mattress and my wall pillow, I feel quite refreshed, and full of very odd ideas. Actually... STOP!

*Everyone does.* TOM *takes a deep breath.*

I've had an idea. I know what I want to do for him.

*Everyone looks at him – a few quizzically – and then set back on their 'Dairylea'.*

MOTHERS.
I tried Edam
I even tried ham
But he said, give me my –
Dairylea (*Repeated in overlap.*)
When I –
Asked him why –
He spat me in the eye. And said –

BOYS (*break from their chorus to sing*).
MUM GIVE ME MY DAIRYLEA,
DAIRYLEA – (*In repeat.*)

DAVID McPHEE, *dressed in a suit, clutching a briefcase, comes in as if being attacked by a hail of bullets. One of the* BOYS *walks slightly too close to him and he flinches away. This is not his natural habitat.*

MOTHERS *re-take song, but it's slower now.*

MOTHERS.
So I do
As I'm told
Wait for him to get old
Prayin' he'll no longer want
Dairylea.

DAVID McPHEE (*muttering to himself*). Go on a site visit they said. Get out of the office they said. Get some fresh air they said. Chance to prove yourself they said. Who knows, maybe tomorrow you'll make us do your photocopying rather than the other way round.

*He bumps into another member of the* SCHOOL CHORUS *and leaps away with a cry.*

I knew this was a bad idea. Of all the places…

TOM. Mr McPhee?

DAVID McPHEE. Arrrgh!

DAVID *jumps two feet in the air, turns pale and starts quivering. Then, looking at* TOM *the entire time, basically moonwalking backwards, he starts unloading things from his pockets.*

Take my wallet. Take my wallet.

TOM. My name's Tom.

DAVID McPHEE. Take the wallet! Just don't – whatever you do – PLEASE DON'T SHOOT ME!

*He drops to his knees.*

TOM. I'm not going to shoot you. I don't have a gun.

DAVID McPHEE. Why would you tell me if you DID?

TOM. Mr McPhee… I phoned and made an appointment…

DAVID McPHEE. TO SHOOT ME!

TOM. Do I really look like someone with a gun?

DAVID McPHEE. Oh, uh… (*Looks up.*) No. You don't really. Actually, you look really like this kid we used to pick on in school… I forget what we called him but by God we gave him hell…

TOM *sits on the wall.* DAVID McPHEE*'s got it in one.*

TOM. Yeah. That sounds about right.

DAVID McPHEE. It was something to do with ice cream, some terribly clever pun on ice cream, eczema and the Irish potato famine… Lord knows why, I don't think he was Irish… … Sorry. For a moment I thought you were one of them…

TOM. One of who?

DAVID McPHEE (*covertly, through his teeth*). Them. THEM. There was a kid got stabbed with a bottle here last week. Them. The ones that killed him. I mean, they could be – oh my God, they could be all around me, levelling their gun sights so as to take a clean shot at me. (*Drops to the floor.*) Take the shot. TAKE THE SHOT. I never should have come...

TOM. So why did you?

DAVID McPHEE *clears his throat and stands up. He hands* TOM *a card.*

DAVID McPHEE. David McPhee, Max Bentley Funeral Homes. You make the appointment. We fill it. Or, rather, we do when we're desperate... We're, um, bit short of business at the moment due to, uh, unforeseen – people are living too long. Horrible business this, uh, healthy living. Now... to business. How can I – ?

*He opens up his briefcase, it explodes everywhere. Papers literally fly out at all angles as if springloaded.*

Oh NO! OH NO NO NO NO NO NO! I WANT TO DIE!

TOM *slaps* DAVID McPHEE, *he's hysterical.*

Ow!

TOM. Better?

DAVID McPHEE. Much. Thanks.

DAVID McPHEE *bends to pick them up.* TOM *helps him.*

So. Really. How can I help you?

TOM. Are you... the work-experience boy or something?

DAVID McPHEE. No – I'm a – that's very insulting – I'm on a modern apprenticeship for undertaking – my mum said there'd always be jobs in death. And after I was expelled from five schools I decided she was right. Sad thing is people seem to be stopping dying. Five a day. Absolute rubbish.

Five portions of chips a day and then we might... DAMN
YOU, JAMIE OLIVER! Anyway, no one else in the office
wanted to come. And for me, it was either this or watch a
body be drained and then filled with embalming fluid. So...
So tell me, what do you want?

TOM. I want to bury my brother. Here. In this pavement.

DAVID McPHEE. Sorry?

TOM. I want to bury my brother – here – in this pavement – here
where he died. I want to bury my brother in the pavement.

DAVID McPHEE *looks down at the pavement and then up
at* TOM.

DAVID McPHEE. Why would you want to do that?

TOM. I just do.

DAVID McPHEE. But – a pavement? You're a boy, is it
really – ?

TOM. I've got money. I can pay...

DAVID McPHEE *hesitates. He licks his lips. He pulls a tape
measure out of his pocket and begins to measure* TOM. *He
turns into a salesman.*

DAVID McPHEE. Would you say he was about your height and
breadth because we've just had a superb new range of
coffins... (*Changes his mind.*) No. What am I saying? No.
*No.* You can't just dig up a pavement and put a body in. You
need to speak to a planner. Get planning permission.

TOM. Planning permission?

DAVID McPHEE. Yes, planning permission. You're digging up
a council-owned pavement. Call a planner. Call your mum.
And, well, it mightn't be a bad idea to call a psychiatrist –

TOM. I'm not mad –

DAVID McPHEE (*interrupting*). And once you have the
permission, from parentals and planners and psychiatrists,
then we'll call Max Bentley Funeral Homes and we'll give
you a quote. You make the call. We fill it.

*He clicks his fingers, puts on a metaphorical hat and exits across the stage.* TOM *is more than disappointed. He lashes out.*

TOM. Mr McPhee? MR McPHEE!

DAVID McPHEE. Yes?

TOM. There's a red spot dancing on the back of your head. Don't look now, but I think it's a gun sight – Mr McPhee, get down, I fear you might be about to be shot.

DAVID McPHEE. Oh… oh… oh… (*Drops to his knees and exits at a fast crawl.*) I never should have come.

TOM *laughs,* DAVID McPHEE *turns round harshly, having realised he's been made a fool of.*

The only people I'm going to tell about this are those that need a good laugh. What kind of freak would want to bury their brother in a pavement, eh? What kind of freak!

TOM *considers the question with a scrunch of his face. Why does he want to bury his brother here?*

**Six**

LUKE *steps out onto the stage past* DAVID McPHEE, *who watches him carefully for signs of violence. When he shows none,* DAVID McPHEE *exits, relieved.*

LUKE *sits down on the wall beside his brother. But* TOM *doesn't notice him.*

LUKE *takes his brother's hand. But* TOM *doesn't notice.*

TOM *just stares forward.*

TOM. We used to have this game we played when we were kids – we'd both be superheroes. I'd be Hero Man, and he'd be Skill Man. We weren't very good with names. And Courtney was the baddie, Super Bitch – though she didn't know she was the baddie, because Courtney wouldn't be caught dead playing stupid games with stupid little kids. Plus, she'd have killed us for calling her Super Bitch. So we used to pretend she knew and hide from her and beat each other up. I mean, really, that was sort of the reason for all of it, a quick game of hide 'n' seek and then a bundle – which generally meant hitting each other. It was good.

I still remember the first time I knew he didn't want me around. The year I skipped was year four. I moved up from the end of year three to the beginning of year five. Anyway, so I was brought in to meet the class, like I was a new kid, though they all knew me because I was Luke's brother from the year below. And then the teacher asked –

*Spotlight on a kind teacher.*

MISS HANDS. Do you want to sit by your brother, Tom?

TOM *stands up, he wiggles from one foot to the next. He's nine years old again.*

TOM. And… And… Luke was sitting by someone else – Ben or someone – and shot me this look. Half-a-smile and half-a-not and half-a-please-don't-sit-by-me-please-don't-sit-by-me. And then he looked away and never looked up. And it sounds stupid now but when you're nine, I mean that was one of the first times I'd figured out that not everyone would like me. You know how you think that? When you're a kid you think 'everyone likes me, of course they do, why wouldn't they? I'm great'. And then you get older and you realise 'no one likes me, of course they don't, why would they? I'm horrible'. Anyway, Luke – that look in Luke's eyes – and then looking away – I knew he'd hate to sit by me… so I sat in the spare seat – beside Martin.

LUKE *starts balancing on the wall behind his brother.*

TIGHT *enters carrying two huge bin bags stuffed with bedding. The midday sun is high in the sky now and* TIGHT *has to shield his eyes from the sun. Not easy, when your hands are full.*

You see, my brother was probably the nicest guy anyone knew – if you'd known him you'd have thought the same – I mean, everyone – EVERYONE – thought he was nice and everyone would say it. Nice Luke. Not that he was that nice, just everyone thought he was. Me, I knew him as he really was –

TIGHT *clears his throat. Both boys twist to see who it is.* LUKE *falls to the ground like a puppet with his strings cut.* LUKE*'s body lies dead on the ground.* TOM *isn't sure which way to look.* TIGHT *makes him nervous.*

I wasn't… talking to myself… I was – okay, I was talking to myself, but there's nothing wrong with that, is there?

TIGHT. Look at the back of my hand. You see hair on it?

TIGHT *charges over and thrusts his hand under* TOM*'s face.*

TOM. Um… I think you mean palm of your hand. The sanity test – whether you can find hair on the palm of your hand – but I'm not mad.

TIGHT. Oh…

TIGHT *looks at the back of his hand and then flips it over. Then laughs.*

Right. Cos there is actually hair on the back of my hand, ain't there? Man, and I thought I was mad. I'll remember that. Palm of the hand. Palm of the hand.

*Pause. The boys make eye contact.* TIGHT*'s permanent smile droops.*

TOM. How did you know Luke?

TIGHT. Yeah. That's what I come to tell you…

*Pause.* TIGHT *doesn't know how to start.*

I ain't goin' to be very good at it. Telling. And you'll probably like – maybe get a bit mad. But – an' it could go quite bad on me if what I say comes out in the whole kind of – wider-world thing.

TOM. I can keep secrets.

TIGHT. Maybe – and maybe you ain't gonna keep this one
secret.

TOM. He was on drugs?

TIGHT. No! Just cos he was coming down here ain't to say he
was into drugs. (*Beat.*) He was in love. Said he was in love.
Went on about it. You know?

TOM. What?

TIGHT. Sorry – love is a bit – rubbish word, innit? But he
really liked saying it… I mean maybe love is alright. No, it
ain't. Cos he didn't mean it. He liked someone a lot. He just
said he loved them. You ain't gonna hit me, are you?

TOM. Who did he like? Who?

TIGHT. Settle. Just – someone he met at the snooker club up
near the town centre. They got talking. They both knew.
Neither of 'em liked it. But they kind of – fell in together…
And then one of them went on about being in love all the
time, and the other was like whatever, and then the one that
went on about being in love got killed with a bottle. Your
brother. You know?

TOM*'s eyes widen, he walks forward.*

TOM. This is… Maybe this is the reason I'm here. Maybe to
find her, talk to her, find out what he was really like. Maybe
the pavement thing is all a – and who cares about solving the
case – I need to find her. You need to help me find her.

TIGHT. Yeah, you see, but it's complicated, you know? Cos she
is a he. I am – it's me.

*Beat.*

TOM. What?

TIGHT. Yeah. This the bit where you could hit me.

TOM. WHAT?

TOM *gets up and walks away from the wall.*

TIGHT. Yeah. I was shocked too. What's it all dem magicians say? Abracadabra. Sorry.

TOM *stands still for a long time – his body static, his mind whirring. Finally he says –*

TOM. My brother was… You're too young…

TIGHT. Same age as you!

TOM. I'm too young. Luke was too young.

TIGHT. For what? For knowing what he was?

TOM. For being in – for liking you. Either of you… you don't… we're too young…

TIGHT (*angry now*). You wanna tell me what I'm feeling now?

TOM. No.

TIGHT. So let me get this right. If I was a girl it was a – 'I need to find her' – but cos I'm a me I'm 'too young, Luke was too young'. And I thought you posh boys was supposed to be – what's the word – open-headed.

*Pause.* TIGHT *controls his anger. This is not the way he wants to go.*

Anyway, whatever, yeah? I'll leave you be, yeah? Just. I bought you blankets. In these bags – and my mum is gonna get well mad cos I didn't ask – cos she don't give blankets to no one who lived on the street and so I nicked them and took them on the bus… I thought you might get cold – at night.

TIGHT *itches his nose with the back of his hand. He's quickly become too scared to look at* TOM, *who is looking at nothing at all.*

We didn't – do sex or nothing – just – kissing and touching and – holding sometimes. I mean, but…

*Suddenly* TOM*'s eyebrows shoot up.*

TOM. Shit! This is a clue!

TIGHT. What? Cluedo for what?

TOM. We need to tell the police – it might explain everything…

*TOM starts to make for the exit.*

TIGHT. What? No. Calm down. Tom. Tom. Where you – ? No, no… you – can't… DON'T.

TOM. I'm going to the station. No, a phone box. Have you got a mobile? What's the number? Stupid me. 999.

*TIGHT shouts after TOM.*

TIGHT. So he was killed by someone who hates gay men? Wow. That is one big clue that, cos most people love gay men. Specially round here. Won't be a clue. Won't be nothing. It'd… it'd… just get me in shit, okay? And your parents, yeah – think about them…

*TOM stops walking.*

You want your parents to find out like this? Thinking they didn't know their son? You want them to? Do you?

TOM (*deeply emotional*). Why not? That's how I feel!

*Pause. TOM turns back to TIGHT.*

Why d'you tell me? I didn't want to know!

TIGHT. I, uh, I – (*Stutter laugh.*) dunno. Seemed right. What? Change how you feel does it? Cos that is –

TOM. Change how I feel? It changes EVERYTHING! We were brothers! We lived together. We went to school together. We were in the same year. I should've known. How did I not know that? Something this big and – I missed it. He should've fucking told me.

*TIGHT hadn't considered this angle.*

TIGHT. Yeah. He should.

*Pause. Both boys are trying to process quite a lot here.*

TOM. You're a coward for not telling the police the truth.
Whether you think it'll change anything. You know they'd
want to know.

TIGHT. Maybe.

*Pause. Neither boy is sure what to do.*

You want these blankets then?

TIGHT *rips open the bin bags, rather too aggressively, and
shovels the blankets out.*

They ain't our best but... And I got you some...

*He hands* TOM *some deodorant – also from the bag.* LUKE
*appears. He watches* TIGHT *carefully, and approaches.*

Just something I noticed... I mean, you stink...

*Pause.*

I ain't a coward.

*Pause.* LUKE *walks up to* TIGHT *and puts his arms around
him, and* TIGHT *melts into him. They stay like that – holding
each other for a few moments.*

TOM. You... you... miss him too?

TIGHT *exits. Not looking back because he's emotional and
doesn't want to show.*

TIGHT. Who d'you think was staking out this wall before you
came dancing?

LUKE *is left onstage with* TOM.

**Seven**

TOM *sits on one of the bin bags. He looks out into the audience.*

TOM. I...

Um... I...

*A GUY on a skateboard rides across the back of the stage – trying an ollie before exiting.*

I just...

*The boy with all the words can't explain himself.*

The thing is, Luke isn't a surprising – wasn't – I mean, that wasn't what Luke – he was straightforward. Not that – not going too far, not doing too much different.

I mean, he didn't –

And I –

*He quietens as a PUSHCHAIR MUM pushes a baby aggressively across the stage.*

PUSHCHAIR MUM. No, what you said was 'get your hands off my remote control, bitch, I got things to do, and people to watch'. I was like – *you* got things to do – *you* –

BABYFATHER. What's with your chatting all the time – chat chat chat... Cos I tell you, I ain't even listening no more...

PUSHCHAIR MUM. You ain't listening? You listen, boy. You listen strong. Otherwise I'm putting that remote control where it hurts and you gonna be birthing it like a baby.

*They exit the stage just as an ESTATE AGENT hurries past.*

ESTATE AGENT (*on the phone*). No, I'm on my way to look at some property on the Tunstall... Lee Marshes... God no, I took the bus, I'm not parking around here – (*Laughs like a jackal.*) well, that's why the first thing I'm going to propose is a garage extension... well, the location is fabulous, that's why... it's called gentrification, darling, and it's happening...

TOM *is still staring into space.*

TOM. I've never liked surprises.

When I was younger, my mum used to have to tell me what was in my presents before I opened them. She knew what I was like.

STAN *comes in wearing a dapper suit. He walks in like the Pink Panther. He has a sort of undeniable slink to him. He's very jazz. The sun is now setting. It's magic hour. And here's the magic man. He has a theme, a light snare drum and some baritone sax.*

I mean... not telling me that. That's – that's spin round five times, touch the floor, bang your head on something... And –

STAN. Hey. Kid. Planning. Me. The cat. Called. You?

TOM *spins to meet his new company. Still totally absorbed by* TIGHT*'s revelations.*

TOM. What?

STAN. You don't talk jive? Thought everyone round here talked jive, man? My name's Stanley Burrows, I'm from the planning department. You called. I came. (*Makes revving noises.*) Grrrm. Grrrm.

TOM. You're – a planner?

STAN. Yeah. Me. Planner. Wow. And you know what – I'm going to make something of this place. Selling it. All. Private development. Tube extensions. Transport links. Wow. Clean. Schmean. Amazing.

TOM *considers what to do.*

TOM. I need your help.

STAN. Who doesn't?

TOM. I want to bury my brother in this pavement. I got told I needed planning permission. Do I? Can you give me permission?

STAN *looks at* TOM, *his eyebrows shoot up. The street lights turn on. One has a bad flicker on it.*

STAN. In the pavement?

TOM. Yeah.

STAN. Wow. Love to, kid. But – jurisdiction. You heard of it? Juris-d-d-d-d-ddiction. This is not a planning matter. This cat keeps his paws clean, you know? Burying brothers in pavements – planning? No, sir. Call environmental health. Call highway control. Nice meeting you. I'm off to prowl. Purrrrrrrr.

*STAN's theme recurs as he sashays his way offstage.*

TOM. Will they let me? Do you think? Environmental... Bury him? Here? In the pavement?

*STAN stops. He turns.*

STAN. Here? Pavement? Grave? Brother? Unlikely.

TOM. Why not?

STAN. Kiddo – schmiddo – huh – you need a good reason to dig up pavements. Not just anyone can do it. It affects people's access – it's a public right of way – you dig?

*He attempts another exit.*

TOM. They dug my street up last week so as to lay a TV cable – you saying laying a TV is more important than burying my brother?

*The flickering street light flickers off. STAN dinks it with the back of his shoe. It switches on again.*

STAN. Which brings me on to – cables and pipes. Gas, electricity, phone lines, cable television, sewers, water, electricity – you open a pavement, there's more cables in there than concrete. Where do you put a dead body? You dig?

*He attempts to make his exit again. This time when TOM stops him, he's annoyed.*

TOM. I don't dig. No.

STAN. Then there's public health – a dead body lives in a whole new way, kiddo. It disintegrates. Disintegrates over our lovely pipes and releases toxins into the atmosphere that really could really jazz up public health. Then there's the smell – I mean environmental health, say hello? Hello. Goodbye. People walk past on a hot day – sun in their face, hope in their heart, they sniff, they think, they say 'What's that smell? Smells like dog meat gone rotten. Oh no, of course it's just that boy's brother disintegrating a bit more.' Sorry. Insensitive. Forget. Brother.

*STAN makes a determined attempt at an exit.*

TOM. Will you talk to other people about it, see if there's any other way…

STAN (*softening slightly, but determined to leave*). What I will do is give you details of a woodland burial ground. Very nice. Classy. Biodegradable.

*He makes for an exit. And this time it's personal.*

TOM. Please… Wait… if I could explain…

STAN. You have explained… Listen, kiddo, I'd love to sit here meowing. But there's mice to be caught, kid. And this cat's gotta catch them.

*He exits across the stage. He stops just as he leaves. He looks around, he smells the air. He sighs contentedly.*

Everything's going to change.

*He exits. There's a final drum kick as he does. TOM watches him go.*

## Eight

*Our* BOY SOPRANO *stands up from behind the wall. He is carrying a glass of water, he thinks about drinking from it, but thinks better of it and hands it instead to* TOM, *who takes it without acknowledgement, drinks a little and then puts it on top of the wall.*

TOM *rips open his bin bags and begins to assemble a bed for the night from the blankets inside.*

*'Tender Contempt'. A lament.*

BOY.
    Lollipops and hairgrips
    Action men and dirt
    Friday-night TV chips
    A water gun that squirts

He –

*The line isn't coming.*

He –

The –

*The* BOY *looks at* TOM. *He doesn't know how to finish this song. Or even sing another line.*

Now he's –

*The* BOY *stops. He can't do this. He walks away.* TOM *looks after him.*

TOM. Second night on the street and it's funny how quickly you adapt to a new life. I mean, I'm not supertramp or – but I am warmer – cos of the blankets – well, that's not adapting, that's just blankets – but the barking dogs bother me less, and the smashing glass and...

I think – I think I was scared of him.

LUKE. You? Scared of me?

    TOM *doesn't hear* LUKE. *And he continues not to do so in the rest of this scene.*

*He continues making his bed. With more gusto now.*

TOM. I wanted him to like me. And I knew he didn't – I knew
he wouldn't – because I wasn't cool like him. I mean, even
using the word 'cool' is probably uncool – I mean, I'm
probably saying it all wrong or using it in totally the wrong
way. I don't know.

There was this big marble competition – the marble wars of
2003 we called it – about three months after I'd joined
Luke's class.

And three months in a nine-year-old's mind is like
unbelievably long. I'd totally settled in by then – which means
I'd been rejected by all the popular people and started musing
with Martin about the kingdom we'd rule called 'computer
club'. And we were far too old for marbles, everyone who
took part – I mean, nine-year-olds, ten-year-olds playing
marbles – what is this, 1950? I mean, literally some kids
played with a fag in their mouth and a knife in their pocket.

LUKE *(laughs)*. Knife? Who carried a knife?

TOM. Still – somehow marbles became important and me and
Martin – we practised loads and we won and kept on
winning – shooting through the rounds – until we got paired
together in the semi and Martin said –

*Light on* MARTIN.

MARTIN. No, this is totally ace, it means a member of the
computer club is guaranteed a place, a grand final. It's like
two English clubs pairing each other in the Champion's
League semi-finals. It's perfect.

*Light off.*

TOM. Neither of us know much about football.

Oh, and he didn't speak to me for a week when he lost.

And then suddenly it was the final – and I was in it.

*'Eye of the Tiger'-type music. Cast from offstage wheel on
huge beach balls done up to look like marbles. The cast are*

*now all in tracksuits and PE uniforms. They look terrible.*
*They start limbering up as if 1970s sportsmen.*

And I was facing – my opponent was – well – as it turned
out – Luke. Of course I'd practised hard to make it to the
final and he was – well, he did it on natural talent.

LUKE *takes a beach ball from one of the cast and lines up*
*his eye.*

He threw the first marble. He looked at me, and then threw
it. And it was – it was –

LUKE *rolls. One of the cast picks up the ball and rolls with*
*it until placing it carefully in the auditorium. There is some*
*sort of musical accompaniment to this. The rest of the cast*
*keep playing games of their own.*

First off I was winning – and then he was – and then me –
and then him – and then – it came down to one large
marble –

LUKE. Was a butterfly marble, I remember it well… I'd won it
in one of the earlier rounds.

TOM.…and I just needed to chink it out of the circle. I won't
attempt to explain the rules – think curling meets lawn
bowls. It was a sophisticated game.

LUKE. We always liked making rules, more than the games
mostly.

TOM. One large marble and all I needed to do was chink out of
the circle – and I'd win…

TOM *picks up a beach ball and lines up his shot.*

…and I let my marble go with loads of wrist spin –

TOM *lets the ball go and similarly it's rolled by a cast*
*member. The cast start paying attention to this battle now.*

LUKE. You always used to talk shit about things like wrist spin.

TOM.…and it rolled and it rolled and it rolled…

*The ball is rolled and rolled and rolled, deep into the auditorium. The cast are now really closely watching this. Think Scotland. Think Winter Olympics. Think curling.*

LUKE. Yours was a speckled hen. Small, compact, usually a good aim...

TOM. And I couldn't look at him and he couldn't look at me.

LUKE. I just, I wanted to beat you at something just once.

TOM. And it rolled...

*The ball keeps rolling.* TOM *is breathlessly watching it. Leaning left to encourage it to do the same.*

LUKE. You won every maths test, every history test. Always top of the class when I'm always in the middle.

*The ball slides past the one already placed. The crowd cheers.* TOM *groans.*

TOM. And it – and it – it slided by on the outside, it nudged but it didn't chink. I should have used a heavier marble –

LUKE. And I won. I beat you. The best. The kid who was younger than me, but always seemed to get there first.

TOM. My wrist spin was all wrong... And all his mates were cheering and holding him up. Chuffed their popular champion has beaten the lonely geek.

LUKE. Popular? Me? They don't even know who I really am...

TOM. And everyone wanted to touch you – to congratulate you – to tell you you're the best. And I don't even have Martin to talk to because he's still sulking...

LUKE. You reckon they'd touch me with a bargepole if they knew I liked boys... I envy you Martin. Martin cares about you. No one cares about me.

TOM. Luke winning was fine... I mean, fine. But he had this flushed look all day – like he was really pleased it was me – and I hated that. I hated that look. That wasn't fine.

LUKE. I loved it. Finally showing you what it was like to lose. Like I had to. Every day.

TOM (*finally spitting it out*). WHY DIDN'T YOU TELL ME WHAT YOU WERE?

LUKE. WHY D'YOU THINK? I needed a brother. And I didn't have one.

TOM. I couldn't talk to you.

LUKE. I couldn't talk to you. And I had more to say.

*This shocks* TOM. *He fades into silence.* LUKE *reaches out to touch his brother. But changes his mind.*

I still remember first day in class the teacher asked if you wanted to sit by me –

*Spotlight on a kind teacher.*

MISS HANDS. Do you want to sit by your brother, Tom?

*Spotlight off.*

LUKE. I knew you'd say no, I had to prepare myself for you to say no, this brother who'd got bought into my class, my world, and I knew you'd…

TOM (*shocked*). No! You gave me a look! You didn't want me to sit by you… You gave me a look…

LUKE. What look? I didn't give you a look, and – you said no, and went and sat by that Martin kid and I –

COURTNEY *enters from beside the stage, and* LUKE *falls to the floor.* TOM *doesn't realise this.*

TOM. Luke… Luke…

TOM *looks around wildly for the reason why his brother – who he's finally been able to talk to – has gone. He notices* COURTNEY *watching him. He looks at her suspiciously. She looks back with equal suspicion.*

## Nine

TOM. Uh. Hi. Um. Hasn't been – three days yet, has it?

COURTNEY. No.

TOM. So how come you're – ?

COURTNEY. I plead temporary insanity – I wanted to check you're okay.

TOM. Oh. Really? Um. Okay.

COURTNEY. I am your sister. I know you like to pretend I'm not. But –

TOM. I'm okay.

COURTNEY. Good. And… uh… well, I bought you some…

*She proffers some blankets at the exact same moment as realising* TOM *already has some.*

Who – got you blankets?

TOM. Just someone… I, just… someone… You wanna sit down? You can see the stars really clearly. Must be cos most of the streetlights are broken round here…

*Pause. She looks at the spot. Realises it's where her brother was murdered.*

COURTNEY. No. I better get back.

TOM (*firm*). Sit down, would you?

COURTNEY. Tom… this is – like a horror movie or something – sitting where he… died.

*She starts to exit briskly.*

TOM (*firmer still*). I want… I don't know enough about you, Courtney… like, what do you like doing? Or what do you think when you meet someone? Or what you want for Christmas? Seriously. STOP. Tell me what you want for Christmas.

COURTNEY *turns.*

COURTNEY. What are we, eleven?!? What do I want for Christmas? What do you care?

TOM. I just do.

COURTNEY. You'll start asking me about my sex life next.

TOM. Please. I wouldn't ask if it wasn't – I just want to know.

*Beat. She considers. She looks at her brother's sincere face. She melts slightly.*

COURTNEY. Okay, maybe, just off the top of my head… um… this is embarrassing, I don't know – maybe, a train ticket, to Paris. You know, Eurostar. You reckon it'd cost too much?

TOM. No.

COURTNEY. I wouldn't want to stay. Just a day return. And not to see the shops or any of that crap. Just to buy some food from the deli or eat maybe in one of the small side-street restaurants or…

TOM. You see, that's really interesting, I'd never have guessed you'd have wanted that…

*Beat.* COURTNEY *sums up some serious courage.*

COURTNEY. Look – I haven't told – anyone this so if you laugh – I want to be a chef.

TOM. Oh.

COURTNEY. You laugh and you'll never have kids, I mean that! I'll do what you did to the dog.

TOM. I'm not laughing. Chef?

COURTNEY. Yeah. Chef. You think I'm mad?

TOM. No.

COURTNEY. Mum'll be well pissed off 'with your GCSEs, chef? But you could do so much better!'

TOM. I like it when you cook for us. Those puddings you do – the cakes… You should make more of them.

*A small smile slides across* COURTNEY*'s face.*

COURTNEY. Okay. Well. Thanks. But… Don't tell anyone, okay?

TOM. No, I won't tell anyone.

*Pause.* COURTNEY *moves across and sits by him, smoothing out the blanket.*

COURTNEY (*soft*). What are you doing here Tom?

TOM (*soft*). I don't know. I just – I wish he'd told me what he wanted for Christmas.

*Pause.* TOM *is thinking – hard.*

The thing is… the thing is, I thought he was stupid.

COURTNEY. He wasn't.

TOM. And I thought he didn't like me.

COURTNEY. I thought he didn't like you too.

TOM. And I thought he was boring. Uninteresting. Not surprising.

COURTNEY. Wasn't he? What was surprising about him?

TOM. I used to think – I was the most special person I knew – which is not – I mean, I thought I was Jesus Christ for a bit but…

COURTNEY. – Jesus Christ?

TOM. – It's a long story. But I always thought – I always felt better than everyone around me. What if – what if Luke was the special one and I was too dumb to –

COURTNEY. What if he was ordinary? Does that make it anyway different?

TOM. No. But he wasn't…

COURTNEY. No… I don't suppose anyone is.

*Pause. Lights fade.*

It's not bad round here really, is it? I mean, it's bad but not as bad as – people say.

TOM. No, it's okay – this woman from the flats even came down with a tupperware dinner for me the other day – rice and chicken.

COURTNEY. That's nice.

TOM. Courtney. Do you ever think – you think death is magical. I mean, not David Blaine or people coming back to life. Just magical – you know?

COURTNEY. I don't know. Shall we go to sleep now, you reckon? Yeah?

TOM. Yeah.

*Beat. In darkness.*

Courtney –

COURTNEY. Yeah.

TOM. Thanks for telling me what you want for Christmas.

COURTNEY. Okay.

TOM. She slept by the wall too that night. And together we braved the pavement elephants that came out to dance –

*An Indonesian shadow-puppet dance starts at the back. A pavement elephant waltzes across it.*

And the sky dragon that came out to sing –

*A burst of flames as a sky dragon coughs.*

And the concrete sabretooths –

*A wide, sharp-toothed mouth cracks down on the assembly.*

And the creeping wall-monkeys that laughed through it all.

*A monkey laugh as they swing mercilessly around the stage.*

And we were too old for all of them. Too old and sophisticated for fairy stories. Because I'd stopped believing when I was six and found my Christmas present from Santa on my dad's credit-card bill. But still – we had to fight the mystical creatures and we did and by the time the sun came up she was gone.

And I felt closer to Luke than I ever had done.

## Ten

*The sun rises and it's beautiful. Gently tinkling the metallic pavement with a soft glow.* LUKE *and* TOM *are sitting leaning their backs against each other.*

*They say nothing.*

*And then a loud* ESTATE AGENT *with an anxious* CLIENT *interrupts the serenity.*

ESTATE AGENT. I think you'll find it a most vibrant place to live.

CLIENT. Well, uh, what's uh – I mean, crime –

ESTATE AGENT. Figures. Schmigures. Breathe. Ingest. Look at this place. It's vibrant, it's exciting, it's new – and that may sound like estate-agent speak, but I'm really excited about where this area can go. And, of course, they're extending the Tube line, you know – which means prices will rocket –

CLIENT. Oh. Well, that does sound interesting –

*The* ESTATE AGENT *and* CLIENT *disappear offstage.* TOM *watches him go.*

TOM. It's funny how things – two days ago I was frightened of this place. Now I'm frightened what it's going to become. Do you know what this place feels? It feels honest. And I know I sound like a patronising wanker even saying… I mean, I'm here for Luke, not for the scenery, but… I don't know, you look behind Batman's mask and sometimes things are better… and this place – well…

*Two* PATROLMEN *walk out onto the street. They're carrying some yellow tape and some traffic cones. They're dressed in riot gear.*

PC BOB. You hot, Bill?

PC BILL. Toasting lightly, you, Bob?

PC BOB. Same as. Same as. Remind me, Bill, why we in riot gear?

PC BILL. Be prepared, Bob. That's the police motto.

PC BOB. No. That's the Cub Scout motto, Bill…

PC BILL. Is it, Bob? What's the police motto?

PC BOB. Dunno, Bill. Think it's in Latin.

PC BILL. You can't even remember it roughly, Bob?

PC BOB. At a guess, Bill, something about attending to needs. We are here today, for instance, to attend to this young man's needs.

*He indicates* TOM.

PC BILL. And what does he need, Bob?

PC BOB. Well, Bill, according to our police report, he wants to bury his brother in the pavement.

PC BILL. Oh, shall I fetch my spade, Bob?

PC BOB. What?

PC BILL. You know, Bob, give him a hand.

PC BOB. No, Bill, we're here to tell him no. And threaten him with arrest. If he stays here and keeps making a public nuisance of himself… we'll arrest him.

PC BOB *starts reassembling the ribbon fence,* PC BILL *dips in to give him a hand. They assemble it around* TOM.

PC BILL. Just a question though, Bob, how is threatening him, attending to his needs?

PC BOB. We're setting him rules, Bill, people need rules, especially people on this estate.

PC BILL. Great answer, Bob. Shall I let him know? About the rules?

PC BOB. Why don't you do that?

PC BILL *ties off the ribbon, approaches* TOM, *bends down, and then shouts in his ear.*

PC BILL. YOU WILL NOT BURY YOUR BROTHER IN THE PAVEMENT. AND YOU WILL STOP MAKING A PUBLIC NUISANCE OF YOURSELF… (*Sniffs, disgusted.*) AND YOU WILL HAVE A BATH… SOON.

TOM. He was gay.

PC BILL. What?

TOM. The victim. My brother. He was gay.

PC BOB. Do you not read the papers, boy? We know he was gay. Everyone knows he was gay. It's common knowledge, the boy was gay. We had a kid come and report it. Might help us find who did it. Probably not. But it was nice to know, wasn't it, Bill?

PC BILL. It was, Bill. Very nice.

PC BOB. What? I'm Bob. You're Bill.

PC BILL. Oh. Yes. That's right. Sorry, Bill.

PC BOB. Bob… Bill… (*Seriously confused.*) What? Listen, son. Just – you can't stay here, okay? Why don't you – go home.

TOM. This is where I belong.

PC BOB. Well, that's not true, unless you're a traffic cone, that is, isn't that right – (*Unsure.*) Bill?

PC BILL. That's right, Bob –

*They both smile – relieved to have got each other's names right.*

Well, that's us. See you, kid. Stay away from the tape. Stay away from the scene.

*They walk past* TIGHT *as he walks onto stage. He scowls at them.* LUKE *follows him onto stage, watching him carefully as he does.*

*Once in the middle of the stage, he checks they've gone, and then begins unravelling the tape.*

TIGHT. Hi.

LUKE. Hi.

TOM. Hi.

TIGHT (*indicating the tape*). Don't want this, do ya? Cos I got a guy in Fulham pay good money for this. I tell you, man, eBay, man, changed my life. But if you – you want it?

LUKE. Do you like him?

TOM. No.

TIGHT. Hey! You weren't talking to yourself when I come out, that's well good, innit.

LUKE. It was his smile got me. He's got a great smile, don't you think?

TOM. No.

TIGHT *has now unravelled the 'police don't cross' ribbon which he then pockets.*

TIGHT. Like this means shit. Like police mean… But. Still. I told 'em. I weren't no coward about it either. I went down in person to tell 'em. Face-to-face. That'll get back that will – people will know it's me… and that'll mean, wreckage, you know?

LUKE. I'm not saying I'd have spent the rest of my life with him… But he's nice, Tom, he's really nice…

TOM. Okay. He's nice. He's nice, okay?

TIGHT. Who's nice?

TOM (*flicked back into* TIGHT*'s world*). What? I was just – I mean, brave, not nice… that was brave. I mean, yeah. Thanks. You're a good – person.

TIGHT (*smiles gently*). Yeah. Well. We ain't all drug dealers round here, you know…

TOM. No. I know. In fact, I can understand why Luke spent time here. I mean, it's quite a nice – I don't know. But it did… kill him, didn't it? This – place. So…

*Pause.* TIGHT*'s face darkens.* LUKE *looks at him apprehensively.*

LUKE. You'll need to listen to this bit.

TIGHT. Yeah. 'Bout that. I don't reckon it was no gay-basher did it.

TOM. Oh.

TIGHT (*gushing out*). Yeah, cos… the thing is… the… I reckon he did it himself.

TOM *looks at* LUKE, *who says nothing.* TIGHT *is finding this very difficult indeed.*

Yeah. Innit. He weren't that happy, your brother, kept going on about how thick he was, and how his life was gonna be shit, and how he couldn't work out how to tell no one what he was, and then I split up with him and the weather weren't great and…

TOM. What? No. He… uh. No. You've got the… He ain't the type.

TIGHT (*barely listening*). I weren't even nice about it. He kept saying 'it's cos you're scared' and I was saying 'you're scared too, you ain't told no one about us' and he was like 'you're scared' he kept on and kept on and kept on and he was right but I couldn't – I wouldn't – so I was like 'that ain't even the main reason, the main reason is you're not good enough for me' and I only said it like that cos I wanted to hurt him and I wanted the conversation done and I knew it would be done then – cos he never did think he was good enough for anyone, did Luke. It's how come everyone liked him. 'Cept you.

TOM *says nothing. He's too busy computing.* LUKE *looks steadily into the distance.*

And now – I need – I need you to forgive me...

TOM. You really think – ? You think he did – himself?

TIGHT. I need you to forgive me...

TOM. Suicide?

LUKE. I'm sorry.

TIGHT....For what I done. I need you to tell me it's okay. Cos I got this cloud, man, and it won't – and I miss him, so bad and... He was right, I was scared, but I proved I can be different now, right? I told everyone – (*Gestures to the paper.*) weren't the coward you said I was. People'll find out was me who told 'em he... you know... So...

LUKE. Tre told me he didn't want to see me again – you hated me – and I was standing in this cold street and I didn't want to go home, I didn't want to do anything. And we'd done that thing in biology about the carotid arteries in the neck and so I broke a bottle and just – and if I'd known how much it hurt... and...

LUKE*'s neck starts bleeding, he puts his hand up to stop the flow.*

TIGHT. Tom – Tom – you gone all quiet, you okay?

*The truth is,* TOM*'s not hearing either of them, he's just got the suicide word rebounding around his head.*

LUKE. I'm not saying – if I had to do it again – if I had to do it again – I mean, it wasn't like I spent my entire time going 'how do I kill myself' because I didn't – just – at that moment – everything seemed right... I wouldn't have done it any other day – or I don't think... It was just – that day – seemed too hard. I just – got a bit crushed and felt a bit – crushed so – crushed myself...

LUKE *takes his hand off, and lets his neck bleed.* TOM *stands up to look at him carefully.*

TIGHT. It ain't your fault, it's mine.

TOM. No.

TIGHT. How can we fix it then? We need to fix it!

*TOM stands in the middle of the stage, finally owning the space around him. His grief has allowed him that.*

TOM. You… You're – the guy that can get anything, right?

TIGHT. Right.

TOM. I – I need an axe.

TIGHT. Is it?

TOM. I need an axe.

*Pause.*

TIGHT. I can get you an axe.

*An axe is bought onstage by a glamorous-looking GIRL (or a boy dressed up). TIGHT catches it. He hands it to TOM.*

*TOM thinks – and then hammers it into the ground. Music starts. Something substantial.*

TOM. It wasn't until the axe hit the pavement that the dance started…

*The glamorous one begins to belly dance. He/she is joined by other brick-wall princesses.*

*TOM hammers it into the ground again.*

It was the brick-wall princesses that started it off – a primative belly dance that shook the room and then the lamp-post monkeys began to wobble and shout…

*The lamp-post monkeys do indeed begin to wobble and shout. It begins to feel epic.*

*TOM smiles and hammers the axe in again.*

*A MAN IN UNDERWEAR comes running on the stage. The music stops. Everyone turns to look at him.*

UNDERWEAR MAN. OI! Don't do that. You know how long it took 'em to get cable put in round here?

TOM *thinks and then hammers again. The music starts up again. Louder, more robust than before.*

TOM. And then the pavement elephants came out to play. And the sky dragons. And the cable moles and the pipe snakes and electric eels.

*And they do.*

UNDERWEAR MAN. Stop. Stop! My sports. My movie channels. Please. I'll do anything. My Granada Men and Motors. My Living TV. My Sci-fi Channel!!!

TOM *hammers again.*

TOM. And slowly – slowly the place became – well, magic.

TOM *hammers again. As the magic and the noise continues all around – slow-fade to a spot on the middle of the stage, in which* LUKE *stands. Still covered in blood.*

TOM *approaches and joins* LUKE *in the spot. They slowly dance around each other, and then slowly* LUKE *droops into* TOM*'s arms. Who stands there holding his brother.*

The night he died – they basically forgot about me. Courtney said she heard Mum crying, and woke then, and came downstairs to find out. But I didn't hear anything. He hadn't come home, I knew that before I went to bed, but I figured he was just with mates, even Mum wasn't worried, so I slept well and slept deep. Anyway, about four a.m. I woke up and I needed a piss, and a glass of milk, so I went downstairs. And Mum was in tears and sitting in a corner of the kitchen on the floor and Courtney was standing crying and Dad was just really really angry – saying things like 'well, what the hell was he doing down there'. And there was a police officer making everyone tea and trying to look unobtrusive and I – was – seeing all this was like – I just – and I didn't know what had happened.

Anyway, so I ask 'what's going on' and they all turn and look at me – and they didn't want to explain it all again – my parents didn't – so the police officer said – because she knew they didn't want to explain it again 'I'll take him in the living room, shall I? Let him know what's happening'. And Mum just nodded.

They'd told Courtney themselves, but that was probably because they knew she'd have a better reaction than me, and they wanted to hug her and stuff. I was never the sort of boy that people hugged, Luke was that sort of boy, I was – I'm the sort of boy people pat. On the back, head, or arm… Anyway, when the police officer told me and I asked 'are you sure' and she said 'that's a strange response' and I said nothing and that I probably needed to go to my room for a bit and she said okay and then I went and sat in my room and played Solitaire on my computer. And –

He's not going to be buried here. They've put him in the ground already. They're hardly going to dig up the body to put in a concrete hole. But this is – my burial, isn't it? The time I'm burying him, for me. And I know him now, and I know what I'm burying and I know what he means to me now, I know that I love him.

You know that, don't you? I love you. You know that? And I'm sorry. I'm so sorry.

COURTNEY *slowly approaches* TOM *and helps him lower* LUKE*'s body to the ground.*

COURTNEY. Yeah. He knows you are.

*Blackout.*

## Epilogue

*A full cast blow-out.*

CHORUS.
Burying your brother in the pavement
Seems such a stupid-weird-thing to do…
But when your mind's a pit
It seems like a bit
Of a way to make things feel less through…

Burying your brother in the pavement
Oh what funny people are we…
But actually it ain't bad
Actually it ain't mad
Just a wave to those we've let free

Burying your brother in the pavement
I got a plot picked out for me
For it's such a way
To deal with the day
When I go on to what may be.

TOM *is placed in handcuffs by* PC BILL *and* PC BOB, *as the chorus sing. He tries to wave goodbye. He's handcuffed. He can't. Everyone else gets their bow.* TOM *runs in as if escaping to take his too.*

**www.nickhernbooks.co.uk**

 facebook.com/nickhernbooks

twitter.com/nickhernbooks